Dinghy crewing

SAIL
TO WIN

Dinghy crewing
Julian Brooke-Houghton

photographs by Tim Hore

Fernhurst Books

First published 1984 by
Fernhurst Books, 13 Fernhurst Road, London SW6 7JN

ISBN 0 906754 16 X

Acknowledgements

Thanks are due to Jimmy King and Peter White for helming the boats
in the photo sessions, and to Milanes and White for supplying the
505. Thanks are also due to the Queen Mary Sailing Club, Ashford,
Middlesex, and the Hayling Island Sailing Club, Hampshire for their
hospitality during the photo sessions.

Permission is gratefully acknowledged to reproduce the following
photographs: pages 11, 15, 50, 57 (top) and 63 (bottom) — Roger
Lean-Vercoe; pages 49 and 59 — François Richard. The cover
photograph is by Tim Hore and the cover design is by Behram
Kapadia.

Composition by A & G Phototypesetters, Knaphill
Printed by Ebenezer Baylis & Son Ltd, Worcester

Contents

Introduction

Many people, particularly helmsmen, cast the crew in a supporting role. They see you as a person who pulls things, moves your weight about and responds to orders. If you are lucky and work hard, the argument goes, you may even be able to helm yourself one day.

But if you look at any successful dinghy you'll see the reality is quite different: the helmsman* and crew work together as a race-winning team. After all a navigator, tactician, foredeck hand, trimmer and helmsman are needed to cope with a large yacht. A modern dinghy is hardly less complex, but all the work and all the information coming aboard have to be 'processed' by just two people. Being short-handed in this way, any helmsman who tries to do everything himself is plainly crazy. Crews *can* think, and in any case two heads are usually better than one in sorting out problems. And let's face it, racing is a pretty complex enterprise at the best of times.

So a good crew needs to have just as firm a grasp of tactics, tuning and weather lore as his helmsman. These topics are well covered in the other *Sail to Win* books. In this book I am going to concentrate on crewing techniques.

Part one explains how to sail the boat fast — skills you can master well before any race begins. I show you how to trim the jib, handle the spinnaker, hike and trapeze. I look at manoeuvres such as tacking, gybing and even capsizing. And I also detail the equipment the crew needs to work the boat properly.

Part two looks at your jobs during a race — from planning the campaign right through to choosing the best end of the finish line. The skills you learned earlier can now be combined to power the boat round the course, and I've added a few specific techniques like accelerating off the start and gybing on windshifts.

I've aimed the book at two kinds of readers.

Publisher's note: "or helmswoman" is implied throughout.

The text and photographs, taken together, will show fairly competent crews how to improve to international standard. But complete beginners can grasp the basics of crewing from studying the photos and their captions: later on they can use the text to help perfect each technique.

Crewing is fun. Carrying out complex tasks really well at the sharp end can give tremendous satisfaction and, if you do them well, will put you in hot demand. Helmsman are always complaining that they can't find a decent crew, and moaning that there are very few about. If you can master most of the things in this book you should be able to take your pick of helmsman. I hope you don't have too much trouble choosing a good one!

Good luck, and enjoy your racing.

Part 1
Sailing the boat

1   The jib

It is a great pity that the jib is so often taken to be the poor relation of the mainsail. In fact the jib is far more sensitive to correct setting, and for its size more effective.

If you look at different classes you will see jibs of all shapes and sizes. Most have the tack at deck level but the clew may be high or low (see figure 2 for parts of the jib). The jib may be tall and narrow or sweep back to overlap the main. All these factors have a bearing not only on the theoretical efficiency of the sail but also on the effect of a small alteration in sheet or halyard tension, or clew position.

In section (figure 1) the sail is generally built to be aerofoil, circular or somewhere in between. The ratio of depth of curve (d) to width (w) increases towards the head. Generally more power is produced by sections which are nearer a true aerofoil and have a higher depth/chord ratio; however, both these factors require the sail to be set at a greater angle to the wind. This means you can either go fast or point high — which we all knew anyway. Any sail is therefore something of a compromise between these conflicting requirements, but it is useful to understand these basic

points before trying to adapt a particular sail to suit the given conditions.

It is certainly possible to pull the sail into a variety of different shapes. The adjustments which affect the basic shape are the tension in the luff and the sag of the forestay or luff wire. The luff wire usually runs through a sleeve in the jib; the tension of the cloth (in relation to the luff wire) is controlled by a lashing at the head of the sail. Although it is possible to adjust the lashing, this is best left to a sailmaker.

So halyard tension only affects the sag in the luff wire rather than the cloth itself. Allowing the luff to sag more by slackening the halyard will add fullness to the front part of the sail, which gives more power at the expense of pointing ability. Tightening the halyard has the reverse effect.

Slots and sheeting

Although the jib is much more efficient for its size than the mainsail, the real advantage of the sloop rig is in combining the two sails. The airflow across and past the jib joins that round the lee of the mainsail to increase the airspeed in this area;

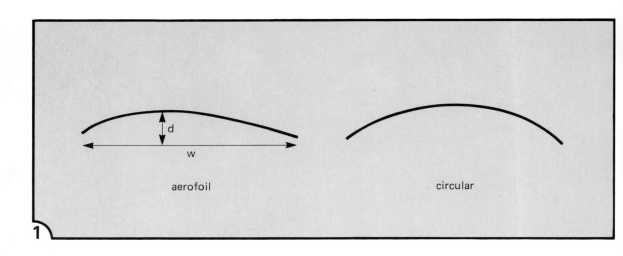

d

w

aerofoil

circular

1

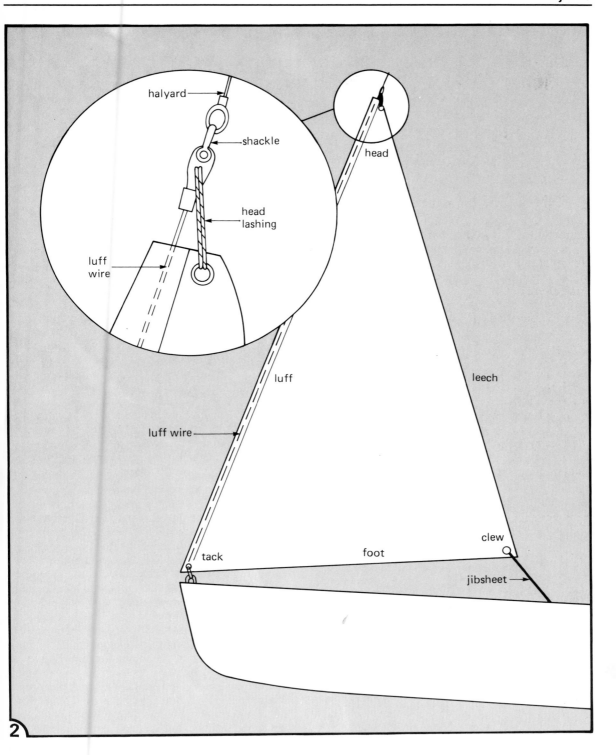

halyard

shackle

head lashing

luff wire

head

luff

leech

luff wire

tack

foot

clew

jibsheet

higher airspeed means lower pressure on the lee side which in turn produces more power from the rig. As the airflow from the jib is brought more into the mainsail flow, airspeed increases until the jib is so close that the flow is constricted, although in many boats the mainsail will already be backwinded by this time. In light airs it is all too easy to choke the slot in this way, especially when trying to point high, because the wind simply doesn't have enough momentum to push through.

This blending of the airflow must be consistent all the way up the leech of the jib, which in practice means that the sail will progressively open towards the head to match the curve of the mainsail, and the luff angle (to the centreline) will also twist a little to match the freeing of the apparent wind which occurs with height above the water. This effect is called wind shear, and varies from practically nothing to 15 to 20 degrees, particularly in light conditions, and is well worth looking for.

A set of three pairs of telltales arranged at quarter, half and three-quarter height will show that the twist is correct when they are all streaming together. If the top leeward telltale is stalled when the bottom ones are streaming, the sail needs to be given more twist by slackening the sheet or moving the lead aft. Conversely if the top windward telltale is lifting when the bottom ones are correctly set there is too much twist — most common when you are close reaching.

Although the finer points of fairlead position, sheeting angle and so forth are well enough covered in books on boat tuning (notably the forthcoming Sail to Win title *Dinghy Tuning*), it is essential that as a crew you appreciate the functions of a jib and the effect of its controls on its performance. It is vital that you can continue to extract the maximum benefit from the sail by changing the settings to match the needs of the moment, which never remain constant during a race. If, for instance, you are set up nicely going to windward in moderate wind and sea and come to a patch of rougher water, the jibsheet should be eased a fraction with the mainsheet to power through, and then tightened again when the patch is passed. Or again, if you need to point up to cover a boat to weather, even at the cost of some speed, just harden in the sheet a little, but don't forget to let it out that bit when you resume your previous course. We are talking about very small amounts of sheet that are eased or tightened,

Above: three pairs of telltales correctly positioned and streaming properly. Opposite, top: tuning against another boat to find the best sail settings. Below: mark each jibsheet to help you maintain a constant setting.

which make a tremendous difference to the sail; the greatest inconsistency in setting comes from inexact sheeting, and the only reliable guide (unless the clew is right by the fairlead) is to have a mark on the sheet which is close to the lead when the sail is hard in which can be seen from the opposite side of the boat. Make sure that the distance from the clew to the mark is exactly the same on each sheet.

Since the setting of the jibsheet is so important, it follows that a reliable means of holding it is essential. Fortunately the days when 'real men' held onto the sheets with their bare hands have gone, and modern cleats are more accurate and reliable than the early models. The siting of the cleats makes more difference than the actual type of cleat, as ideally the cleat should catch the sheet when required and interfere with it as little as possible otherwise. Correct siting gives easy use of the cleat when needed — mostly after a tack or on a three-sail reach — and minimum problems when the trim is being constantly adjusted as on a two-sail reach; in this respect it is better to keep the cleat as far from the last lead as possible. Whether or not you go as far as putting the cleat on the weather side is a matter of choice, but unless you are certain to spend most of your time out over the weather side, I think this is unlikely to be very easy to use in a tack.

Reaching

The attention to detail in setting and adjusting the jib which is so vital when going to windward cannot be forgotten as soon as you bear away. As long as there is smooth airflow round the lee side of the sails there is benefit to be gained from the slot effect, although it becomes less marked as the reach becomes broader.

The extent to which a true slot can be maintained depends on the width of the sail and the clew height. Wide jibs and genoas become deeper and deeper in section as the clew moves forward rather than out, breaking up the airflow off the sail, and there is very little that can be done to alleviate the problem other than partially furling the sail. The high-clewed jibs popular in the '50s and '60s, whilst not as efficient upwind as today's deck sweepers, did not twist off so dramatically at the head when the sheet was eased and therefore were more powerful on a reach. Were, that is, until dinghy sailors discovered the barberhauler, first used on Stars in the 1930s. This device is a ring or block running on each jibsheet, led through a point on the lee gunwale some way forward of the usual fairlead, and controlled from the weather side. By thus taking the sheet to a new lead position — or (more correctly) range of possible positions — the optimum section and twist in the jib

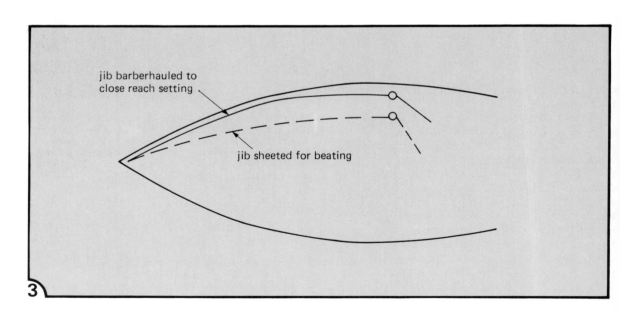

jib barberhauled to close reach setting

jib sheeted for beating

3

can be maintained as the boat is sailed further off the wind (figure 3).

Whilst the possible range depends on the available beam outboard of the windward sheeting position, the fore and aft location of the barberhauler lead is fairly critical; it is better to have it more forward than aft because twist can be increased by easing both the sheet and barberhauler should the lead be too far forward, whereas if it is too far aft you're stuck with too much twist for certain points of sailing. Remember that the barberhauler is not an 'on and off' control; it is to be used carefully in conjunction with the sheet to give as uniform a slot as possible. In some conditions it may even be necessary to apply very subtle amounts of barberhauler when sailing to windward

The effect of jibsheet tension. Above, left: the slot is closed, killing speed. Centre: easing the sheet brings the jib leech perfectly parallel with the main. Right: over-easing loses drive in the upper part of the rig. The mark on the jibsheet shows how little it has moved to cause these effects.

if the jib leads are fixed in one position.

Since the apparent wind direction and the boat's course both vary more off the wind, the jibsheet should be worked continually to keep the telltales flying, unless you have the spinnaker up when you will be too busy. Large sheet movements could also need some adjustment of the barber-hauler to maintain the slot, but the set-up usually accommodates a fair amount of sheet movement without any problem. In heavy or squally weather, let out plenty of sheet when a gust hits to give the boat a chance to accelerate and increase its own stability, and the helmsman a chance to bear off with the boat still level. Then sheet in again almost immediately to pick up speed; the helmsman will (or at least should) ease the main out at the same time. This momentary dumping of the sheet helps to keep control of the boat and costs far less speed than a screeching helmsman with the tiller up to his ears, but it requires practice to judge the amount of sheet to let out and the rate at which to draw it in again.

If you are using the jib and spinnaker together, the latter will take almost all your concentration and effort and the jib will have to fend for itself. Above all it must not be allowed to interfere with the spinnaker, which it will do most on tight reaches when the two luffs are closest together. If you suspect that the erratic behaviour of the spin-naker is caused by the jib, either furl the jib, ease the sheet well out, or drop the sail altogether; genoas can be partially furled to advantage in moderate winds, although the furling gear is not really designed for it.

Do not try to keep the jib drawing perfectly when the spinnaker is flying — it won't. Keep it a little overeased to be certain of smooth airflow and allow for variations in apparent wind direction without constant re-trimming of the sheet. In rough conditions the jib can pin the boat down, preventing the helmsman bearing off enough even though the main and spinnaker are eased well away, so ease the jibsheet even more in these conditions.

Running

On a dead run or very broad reach the jib will be blanketed by the mainsail and will draw more effectively on the weather side. If this point of sailing is going to continue for some time it will

Spinnaker reaching with the jib well eased. Note how far aft the crew has moved to stop the bow burying, having to brace himself against the helmsman to resist the forward pull of the trapeze (see chapter on boat balance).

be worth setting the jibstick (whisker pole, call it what you like) to hold the clew out on the side opposite the main (figure 4). Sheet fairly hard against the pole to limit the twist in the sail. There will be some airflow across the sail from leech to luff, but basically you are trying to create the largest possible obstruction to the wind.

As the wind comes round more onto a broad reach, the jib will eventually be backed and will be pushing the boat the wrong way. Ease the sheet forward to prevent this until the wind is sufficiently abeam to fill the sail properly to lee-ward.

The whisker pole usually hooks onto an eye on the mast. The eye should be reasonably high to push down at the clew without giving away too much radius at the pole end. The other end either has a spike to go into the clew ring or — better — another hook to go over the sheet. The pole is first attached to the sheet or clew, and then pushed out against the tension on the sheet, which you are still holding, and clipped onto the mast. The sheet is best controlled by the helmsman, who should be sitting up to weather to have the best all-round vision, while the crew traditionally leans on the main boom.

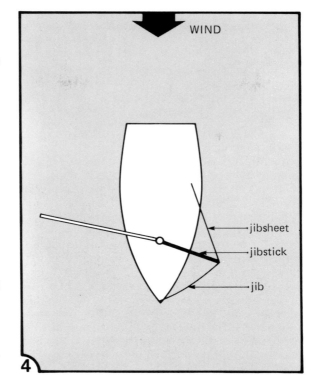

Care of the sail

The jib can be instantly disfigured by kinks in the luff wire, and not improved by creases in the window (assuming you have one) or in the re-inforcing patches at the corners. All these things can be avoided by folding the sail properly when you put it away — coil the luff as you would any other length of wire, rolling the sail into a tube, which can if necessary then be folded round the flat coil of the luff wire. If, however, the jib is made of a Mylar laminate or stiff yarn tempered cloth, it must be loosely rolled round the luff wire and kept in a tube.

However, all the careful folding will be wasted if you leave the sail flogging, knocking all the filler out of the cloth and throwing away its stretch resistance. At the start of a race there are bound to be times when you have to let the jib fly for a while, but a slight tension on the sheet helps to preserve the material without producing any for-ward drive. At any other time the sail should be furled or stowed rather than left flapping.

Opposite: furl the jib as soon as it interferes with the spinnaker — particularly on a run or when in light airs.

2 The spinnaker

The spinnaker, unlike the mainsail and jib, is supported only by the airflow within it. Consequently it must be watched continuously if it is even to stay set; for optimum performance it must have your complete and undivided attention from the second it goes up until it is stowed again.

Early spinnakers were made on the principle that the biggest obstruction to the wind would drive the boat fastest, but we now know that the airflow is basically across the sail, and therefore that better flow can give extra power to compensate for a smaller total area. This trade-off between efficiency and area is being explored in a number of classes, and although the conclusions are hard to separate from pure fashion, it is clear that in classes such as the 505 and International 14 which allow really big spinnakers, biggest is *not* the best.

Modern spinnakers are variations on the spherical cut in which the design shape is a part of the surface of a sphere — of large radius (for flat sails) or small (full sails) — which gives a good symmetrical shape. This symmetry of the basic shape is important because the luff on one gybe will become the leech on the other; we discuss ways of modifying the shape later on.

The cross-cut construction, with all the panels running horizontally across the sail, is most common in dinghy spinnakers where the loads do not cause too much distortion. Since cloth is strongest either along or across its length, and weakest on the diagonal (bias), other cuts have appeared which have triangular panels radiating from the clews, head or all three (the triradial) to overcome distortion in those areas where it was excessive.

Improvements have been made in the weaving and finishing of the cloth which reduce the necessity for these more expensive constructions, or alternatively permit lighter cloth to be used.

One last point — never, *never* dry a spinnaker by hoisting it, pulling down on one clew and allowing it to flap in the wind. Nothing destroys a sail more quickly. The proper way to dry it is to hang it from the head and two clews together, preferably somewhere quiet; if you cannot do that, no harm will be done by leaving the sail wet and drying it in use just before the next race.

Spinnaker gear

Stowage.   Spinnakers are stowed either in the front of the cockpit or in a chute. The chute is a long tube with a bellmouth forward of or alongside the jib tack into which the spinnaker is drawn by a retrieving line attached to the middle of the sail on the outside. Sometimes the tube is shortened or dispensed with altogether and the sail pulled through just a bellmouth, depending on the size of the sail and the boat's buoyancy arrangements. The retrieving line is usually the end of the spinnaker halyard, which keeps the bottom of the boat free of lengths of string. The chute is a very quick way of hoisting and (more particularly) dropping a spinnaker and therefore keeps the boat at speed that fraction longer, which can be very useful at the leeward mark.

Where the spinnaker is stowed in the cockpit, it is best kept in an open bag or basket, which should have drain holes in the bottom and clips for the sheets and halyard to prevent the sail being dragged out unintentionally, for example by the lee sheet trailing in the water. Cockpit stowage is not so slick as a chute, but it does keep the sail much drier when sailing in waves, and avoids the weight of a chute and sodden sail in the bow. It is also the only way to stow ultra-light sails which would tear in a chute, and for very hard, crackly cloth like Dynac which sticks to the inside of the chute.

Halyard.   Use a strong, stretch-resistant line for the halyard, of as small a diameter as possible for free running. Kevlar rope is excellent for this purpose, fulfilling these conflicting requirements, although care must be taken with the leads to avoid crushing the rope. The top sheave cage in particular must be well rounded around the rope

uphaul

pole

sheet

guy

downhaul

Spinnaker gear.

exit to give a good lead when the sail is pulling out to the side; better still, fit a bull's eye or a small swivelling block just below the top sheave, if it is allowed in the class rules.

Wherever it is stowed, the spinnaker is best hoisted by the helmsman, so the halyard (and for that matter the retrieving line) must be led so that nobody can stand on it.

Pole. The pole is used to hold the windward clew away from the mast and to control its height;

it needs to be set, gybed and stowed instantly and faultlessly even in the worst conditions. There are dozens of spinnaker pole systems which are good in some of these respects and not so good in others; the best system for you will depend on the sort of sailing you do, the layout of the boat, the relative length of the pole and, of course, how much string you like to have.

Sheet and guy. The rope should have minimal stretch and small diameter to run freely, and additionally to avoid dragging the clew of the sail down in light weather. However the load on the sheet is often fairly high, and the sheet will be worked continually, so the middle section which is actually held should be thick enough for comfort; this is why tapered sheets have become standard equipment on all the top boats. We refer to the sheet and guy individually, although one length of rope is used to make handling much easier and save weight (wet rope is surprisingly heavy); and then of course you never lose the end.

There must be a way of holding the guy down to the gunwale around the shrouds, particularly while reaching, so that the crew can sit out or trapeze beyond it. This is done either with a simple hook well fastened, or one of the alloy Clam cleats with an open side, so that the guy is adjustable at that point. Alternatively a block running on the guy can be used, pulled down to a lead and cleat on each gunwale; the twinline, as this is called, is continuous from side to side so that it can be adjusted more easily.

There should also be a pair of cam cleats in the cockpit for the sheet and guy; a good location is above the final lead so that the guy can be pulled up into the cleat from the weather side while the sheet is played, and yet both can be cleated for gybing.

Hoisting the spinnaker

From a spinnaker chute.   Assuming you have just rounded the windward mark, ease the jibsheet well out and raise the centreboard to the reaching position. Now pick up the pole, attach the guy and uphaul/downhaul, and set the pole onto the ring on the mast. If the pole has the usual hook end with a plunger in the line of the pole, remember to set it so that the hooks open upwards, which prevents the guy jamming in the piston and makes it easier to remove the pole later on.

Pull in about a metre of sheet as the helmsman starts to hoist; this helps to get the body of the sail moving out and to leeward, and by taking some of the strain off the halyard avoid distorting the head of the sail.

If for some reason the guy is not already through the reaching hook and set to the correct position, which you have conspicuously marked, hook it and set it like lightning before sheeting in to trim the sail, balancing the boat as you do so. If the

Above and right: raising the spinnaker from a chute.

guy is preset, which on the first reach it should be, the helmsman can start to sheet in as soon as the pole is set; doing so beforehand makes it very difficult to push the pole far enough forward to go on the mast ring.

If your boat has an automatic pole launching system, the guy should be in the end of the pole and the uphaul/downhaul is permanently attached. The sheet should still be pulled a little as the sail starts to go up, followed by the pole setting line and finally the sheet trimmed.

From the cockpit. This is quite a straightforward operation when the sail is to leeward, although practice is important to make it as slick as possible. For the first hoist of a race, the spinnaker should always be to leeward because you should be able to decide before the start which will be the first spinnaker leg and therefore which side the sail should be packed. As before, the jib should be eased and the centreboard raised at the windward mark as part of the rounding manoeuvre, before starting to hoist the spinnaker.

First unclip the halyard and sheet and pull out a handful of sail as the helmsman begins to hoist. Then quickly pick up the pole, put the guy into the pole end, fit the uphaul/downhaul and set the pole on the mast. Trim the guy to the correct

Opposite and above: raising the spinnaker from the leeward bag.

position as the helmsman gathers in the slack sheet, take the sheet from him and set the sail, balancing the boat as you sheet in. Quite apart from putting strain on the guy, pulling in the sheet too much before the guy is set will stop the boat dead because the sail will probably be pulling aft and blocking any airflow from the main and jib.

When the sail is stowed on the windward side

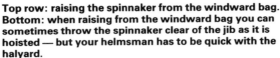

Top row: raising the spinnaker from the windward bag.
Bottom: when raising from the windward bag you can
sometimes throw the spinnaker clear of the jib as it is
hoisted — but your helmsman has to be quick with the
halyard.

the sequence is slightly different, and speed is far
more critical to avoid the sail being blown between
the main and jib as it goes up. A good technique
is to fit the guy to the pole first and hold the guy
and pole firmly in one hand to keep the sail close
to the pole end. Now, pull a handful of the sail
out of the bag as the helmsman starts to hoist,
and using the pole in both hands rather like a
pitchfork scoop some air into the sail and carry it
past the forestay. It is essential to get all the spinnaker luff past the jib in one sweep, and this is
easiest when the sail is not fully hoisted, so you
will have to be quick. If some of the sail is still
stuck on the jib, a second sweep should clear it
easily. Once the sail is to leeward, fit the uphaul/
downhaul and attach the pole to the mast, set the
guy and trim the sheet as before.

Reaching with the spinnaker

Whilst in theory it is possible to work both the sheet and the guy all the time, in practice there is a point beyond which an attempt to adjust the guy is impractical when the wind is forward of, or in stronger winds just aft of, abeam. For our purpose in discussing spinnaker technique we can define reaching as any direction of apparent wind where this applies.

A good spinnaker will allow the luff to flicker and curl before the sail collapses completely, and the fundamental principle of spinnaker trimming is to keep the sail on the point of curling all the time. This is done by gently easing the sheet until a curl begins and then trimming a little, before easing again and trimming, a continuous movement which demands full concentration from the crew. Remember that the aim is to guide the airflow across the sail and past the lee side of the jib (if set) and mainsail; the flow on the lee side of the spinnaker is as important here as the flow on the lee of the main and jib when on the wind.

HALF NELSON

Oversheeting will stall the flow on the lee side and choke the slot between the spinnaker and mainsail, and must be avoided — unless of course you *want* to slow the boat to avoid establishing or losing an overlap at a mark.

The jib, if set, should be eased slightly beyond its normal position because any tendency to stall will produce eddies which will upset the spinnaker, particularly in light winds. In heavier winds the jib should be eased still further so that it is not oversheeted when the boat has borne away down a wave or in a gust; nothing is worse than to bear away in a gust, only to be driven into the water however much the main and spinnaker are eased because there is too much power in the jib. If the boat has a large overlapping genoa, this should be partly or fully furled to take up the 'hooking' which develops at the clew as the sail is eased.

In *light winds* the principle is the same, but it is also important to move as gently as possible in the boat so as not to shake the wind out of the sails; the action of easing and trimming the sheet is therefore more gentle, but just as vital. A slight heel to leeward will help to keep the spinnaker away from the boat, which helps the air escape from the sail.

In *strong, gusty winds* the sheet must be eased in each gust; you will feel the gust go past your ears before it reaches the sail, and should be able to ease the sheet as the gust strikes, keeping the boat upright and the helm light. Much more sheet can be eased than you might think because the helmsman will bear away in the gust and the apparent wind will move aft more as the true wind increases relative to the boatspeed. The spinnaker itself will be more stable in stronger wind, so do not be afraid of easing a good length of sheet, and then trimming in again as the boatspeed and stability pick up. Similarly in *waves*, a quick ease and re-trim as the stem starts to lift will accelerate the air in the sail by letting it out, and direct more of the thrust from the sail forwards, giving an extra burst of power when you need it.

Pole height.   Correct pole height is a key element in the control and performance of the spinnaker;

Left: to remove a twist pull down on the luff and, if necessary, the leech as well. Opposite: in a gust ease the spinnaker sheet as the helmsman bears away.

the simplest 'correct' position is where the curl induced by easing the sheet occurs evenly all up the luff. A lower pole will give more curvature in the forward part of the sail, which gives more stability for sloppy water or when there are holes in the wind and arguably a little more power when reaching. A higher pole reduces the curvature near the luff, which makes it easier to point close to the wind, but tends to put the shape into the leech area which then acts more as a brake; if you need to point up a little to make a mark it would be better to raise the pole briefly rather than take the spinnaker down.

Classically the pole height was set to keep the clews level, which rather misses the point of controlling the performance of the spinnaker. If the pole height is set as described, we should logically consider the clew height in relation to it, and therefore the sheeting position.

The axiom of keeping the clews level can be amended to one of keeping the luff and leech lengths equal, so that if the pole is relatively long, as for instance in the 505, the clew will in fact be lower than the tack, and the sheet lead forward of the transom. Having the lead too far aft results in the bottom of the sail being stretched out on a close reach, and control of the upper part of the sail being lost. Having the lead too far forward on a reach will give a full sail with a closed leech, which is even even worse. For a start, place the lead so that the sheet rises at about 45 degrees when the spinnaker is sheeted as close as you can sail with it.

Centreboard. For close spinnaker reaching the centreboard should be right down until the boat is beginning to be overpowered. The addition of a spinnaker roughly doubles the sail area and when reaching the majority of the thrust is across the boat, so full board is needed to stop the boat sliding sideways. Quite apart from making the boat feel soggy, insufficient board forces the helmsman to head up to achieve the course, so that the sails are all crammed in trying to point when they should be eased out and driving the boat forward.

As the breeze increases the board will have to be raised to lose some of the power and stop the boat tripping over, but the extra speed will make the board more effective so that the actual course will be much the same.

Gybing centreboards are a menace when reaching and running — the effect is like driving a car with a slack steering. If you are convinced of their advantages for windward work, remember to wedge the board downwind, particularly in waves, if only by jamming your foot against it.

The crew's efforts should be devoted entirely to driving the boat as fast as possible with the spinnaker, which is the most important sail once it is set; you should therefore be where as much spinnaker can be seen as possible, and yet in a position to respond to the movement of the boat, wind and waves.

Running with the spinnaker

The spinnaker guy, fixed when reaching, becomes the focus of the crew's attention on the run. The sheet should be used to control the basic shape and fullness of the sail; the guy should be pulled gently aft until the luff begins to curl, and then eased forward before being pulled slowly aft again in a continuous motion. This technique is similar, but opposite, to the use of the sheet when reaching. The easiest way of working is to cleat the guy around its reaching position, put it in the reaching hook, and pull aft on the part between the hook and pole; this gives a more comfortable grip on the rope and also means that the sail can instantly be set for reaching if a luff is needed to pass or respond to another boat.

The spinnaker pole height is again set so that the luff of the sail curls evenly along its length. The effect of a lower pole is to make the sail fuller and therefore more stable, whereas a higher pole gives the boat more life but demands greater skill to control the boat in a breeze. Particularly in sloppy water and light wind the pole should be lower than normal and the sail set further away from the boat. In stronger winds both sheet and guy should be pulled in to flatten the sail slightly,

Left: pole height. In the picture at far left the pole is too high — the luff curls at the bottom first. In the centre, the setting is correct — the luff curls evenly along its length. Near left, the pole is too low — the luff curls at the top first. Below: if the spinnaker sheet is over-eased the leech opens too much and the boat rolls to weather.

and great care taken to keep the sail pointing in the required direction with the boat underneath it; in these conditions it helps to pull the sheet down with the twinlines if fitted, or even put the sheet under the reaching hook on the lee side.

If you cannot furl the jib, pull in just enough sheet on the lee (mainsail) side to stop it being blown out to windward and interfering with the spinnaker.

Gybing the spinnaker

Gybing from run to run.   Because there is usually no rush and little change in the balance of the boat, a gybe from run to run is the easiest to do, and the best start for gybing practice. Of all the spinnaker operations, gybing shows the biggest

improvement for a little practice and quite apart from the satisfaction of a good gybe in difficult circumstances, confidence in your gybing technique enables you to take tactical initiatives downwind.

For most of the manoeuvre the pole will be on the 'wrong' side of the sail, so take your time and do not stampede around the boat shaking the wind out of the sails. The essential point is to bring the spinnaker round to the old weather side before gybing the main, and subsequently to steer to keep some wind in the sail while the pole is being changed over.

Pull in the guy and ease the sheet as the boat bears away, taking the guy out of the reaching hook if necessary (or release the weather twinline and pull in the leeward one). Cleat both sheet

Above: a run-to-run gybe with a single-ended pole. The pole is taken off and stowed, leaving the spinnaker to fly free. The main is gybed, the pole clipped onto the new guy and reset on the new side.

and guy just before pulling the main boom over. When the boat is steady, move to the mast and change the pole onto the new guy. Put the guy under the reaching hook, pick up the new sheet and carry on working the sail. Practice will teach you just where to cleat the guy and sheet so that the sail stays set throughout the gybe, although it is unlikely that the change of course (and hence the cleating point for the sheet and guy) will be the same for every gybe on a run, so it is not really worth marking the ropes at any particular point.

If you have a single-ended pole, or a twin-pole system, the pole must be taken off the old guy just before the main boom comes across, and re-set once the boat is steady. These systems stow the pole along the main boom, so make sure that the main is sheeted in slightly to avoid trapping the pole against the shroud.

When the jib is not furled during a gybe, uncleat the jib sheet before starting to gybe and leave it slack; after the main boom has gone across, push the jib to leeward as you go to change the pole, but do not sheet the jib until the spinnaker is sorted out on the new gybe.

Gybing from reach to reach. The principles and method of gybing from reach to reach are exactly the same as gybing from run to run. There is, however, far more emphasis on speed and balance, and less on keeping the sail full. Despite that, nothing can justify the style of some helmsmen, even eminent ones, who persist in pulling the tiller hard up at the gybe mark and bawling out the crew for the ensuing shambles. Speed is not only an advantage in relation to the competition, it is also much less effort to perform the operations before the sail has really filled on the new gybe; setting the pole and putting the guy under the reaching hook are both far easier without the full load on the sail.

It is still essential to bring the spinnaker round to the old weather side as the boat bears away, and the old sheet/new guy can now be cleated at its mark because the setting for a reach is always the same. The old guy/new sheet will need to be pulled in by a corresponding amount so that the sail is roughly set on the new gybe.

To improve your gybing technique from reach to reach, start by gybing on a run and progressively increase the angle through which the boat is turned until you are gybing from a close reach to a close reach; when chaos develops, go back to a smaller angle and slowly increase again. Before long, you will be the one gybing neatly at the mark and passing to weather of the bunch struggling with their spinnakers.

A reach-to-reach gybe: see text on this and previous pages.

Dropping the spinnaker (but not in the water)

Into a chute.   In theory returning a spinnaker to the chute is simply a matter of letting everything go and pulling the retrieving line, but there are a couple of points which make dropping and subsequent rehoisting easier.

1   As the helmsman releases the halyard and starts to pull on the retrieving line, take the guy and pull the sail square across the boat, easing (but not releasing) the sheet as the sail is drawn into the chute. This collapses the sail, taking the load off the retrieving line, and feeds the sail evenly into the chute.

2   Release the pole from the mast, uphaul/downhaul and guy — in that order — relatively late, so that the sail feeds into the chute from above instead of being dragged over the deck. If there are any waves likely to go down the chute, uncleat the guy as well so that the sail can be pulled right back in the chute; most of the water will then go down the chute drain without soaking the sail. Be sure to keep your feet off the halyard and retrieving line if you value your ticket!
   If the jib was furled on the previous leg (when the spinnaker was set) it should be unfurled and set well-eased before dropping the spinnaker.

Into the cockpit.   The spinnaker is almost always dropped and repacked on the weather side, even though this may mean hoisting again on the weather side, because it is so much quicker than dropping it to leeward. The procedure is very much a reversal of hoisting.

1   Come into the boat, easing the sheet and, if set, the jibsheet.

2   Release the spinnaker sheet; remove the pole from the mast, uphaul/downhaul and guy — in that order — keeping hold of the guy, and stow the pole.

3   Gather the foot of the sail almost as far as the clew and (assuming that the helmsman releases the halyard at this point) stuff the sail into its bag by taking the bunched part in hand over hand. Leaving the clew and leech out of each successive handful should keep the sail free of twists for rehoisting; remember also that the higher you reach for the next handful, the quicker you will gather in the sail.

   Finally clip the guy and halyard to prevent their dragging the sail out again, tidy the sheets out of the water and trim the jib as you round the mark.

Top row: dropping the spinnaker into a chute.

Above and right: dropping the spinnaker into a bag.

3 Boat balance

Traditionally the prime function of a crew has been to keep the boat upright, particularly in a breeze. Leaving aside the historical reasons for such a limited concept of crewing, it remains true that whatever else a crew does (and however brilliantly) the balance and spirit of the boat must be maintained primarily by him or her. If you cannot achieve this, then perhaps you should try helming.

The word 'balance' unfortunately implies a static and stable situation, whereas a sailing dinghy reacts in an almost animate way to continuous variations of wind and water, requiring a live and often subtle response from the helmsman and crew to achieve the best performance. Sympathetic body movement is a vital part of good boat handling and speed, developed by understanding and experience. You must maintain a live, fluid movement to anticipate and respond to the effect of wind and waves (and tactical situations with other boats), constrained only by the extremes of sitting out or trapezing and the boat's layout and other occupants. As far as the class rules allow, the arrangement of the boat should make it possible to move around easily, and the controls and leads should be sited so that they can be used from almost any position.

Despite this concept of mobility much of your time will be spent well outboard of the boat, more or less in one position, with only limited body motion being needed; response is still important for performance — a sandbag over the gunwale just doesn't have the same effect — but the scale is smaller. We therefore look at this sitting out (or hiking) position before going on to consider trapezing as an alternative.

Sitting out/hiking

Whilst you may briefly be able to hold yourself horizontal with your knees on the gunwale, even masochists will agree that this diverts much of your concentration from the race in hand. The classic position where the knees are some way inboard of the gunwale and as bent as possible has evolved as the best compromise between leverage and agony. To maintain your position you must keep within your limits of muscle power and stamina, joint strength and blood circulation.

The strain on the thigh muscles can be reduced by moving your feet down and outboard as far as the structure of the boat will allow, but this increases the load on your knee joints unless you also move inboard, which is not the idea at all. You will have to experiment to find the position between these two effects which suits you best.

The strain on the stomach muscles is directly related to how flat you hold your torso. I think it is best to keep the maximum effort here for times of urgent need, e.g. at the start, and to adopt a slightly more relaxed position generally, which leaves scope for some dynamic response to waves and gusts of wind. Sometimes it is a help to hang on the jibsheet provided you can hold it above the gunwale, but watch you don't change the jib setting by doing this.

Blood circulation can be a problem when you put a lot of pressure on the back of your calves and thighs by a combination of sitting out too far, carrying too much weight, and bad design of the side decks. The first two are your own problem, but you may be able to spread the weight over as large an area as possible (look carefully at the class rules) and could also use some sort of stiff padding such as soccer shin pads to similar effect.

The straps themselves should be flexibly woven without being too stretchy, the soft weave allowing them to conform to your ankles; some people like to wrap them with foam pipe insulation for even greater comfort. The straps must be held off the floor with shock cord — not rope — so that you can stand on them without breaking anything, and be fastened very strongly with a decent spreader plate on top of the webbing. They need to extend far enough fore and aft to allow you to trim the boat properly, bearing in mind that as

Good hiking technique.

you come aft when reaching you will also want to sit higher to clear the waves, and that if the straps are too far outboard you will have difficulty getting your feet in and out of them quickly, with entertaining results (for everyone else).

Trapezing

The trapeze is an ideal way of extending the working range of a crew, or for that matter a helmsman, to increase the available power without increasing weight. The scope for movement outboard is much greater both across the boat and fore and aft than it is inboard, and movement is much easier and smoother and needs less physical effort.

The principle is simply that the body weight is taken by a wire attached to the mast at some point around the hounds; systems to make use of the idea are a little more sophisticated, and we can consider each item in detail.

Wire attachment to mast. 2.5 mm diameter 1 x 19 stainless wire is quite adequate, and can be attached directly to the mast or very carefully to the shroud itself. Fixing to the mast is more reliable, and can be used to vary the bend in the topmast depending where the wire is attached; the neatest method is for the wire to pass through the mast wall and have a soft eye round a tube passing athwartships through the mast — T terminals are quite capable of jumping out if there is no load on them. The benefit of swaging the trapeze wire onto the shroud clear of the mast is reduced windage in the critical area around the mast, but it must be done very carefully to avoid crippling the wires which will then fail after some use.

Handles.   The handle should be just high enough for you to be able to lift yourself when sitting on the gunwale; any higher is more difficult to reach when right out flat, and any lower makes it harder to get in and out. The triangular type of handle is better than the T shape, because the four fingers are not equally strong.

Ring.   Two position rings are standard equipment, the longer (lower) part being used when you are continually right out on the trapeze, and the shorter (higher) when you are not always trapezing or are just outboard for a long period. The ring is attached to the handle by a strop which should be rope to give the system some shock-absorbing capacity. The strop may be adjustable for length with a jamming block, but if you are

regularly crewing the same boat you will probably find that changing from the long to the short ring, and vice versa, is enough and the strop need not be altered. You can then reduce windage by replacing the purchase with a simple length of rope spliced onto both the ring and handle. The length is of course absolutely critical.

Shock-cord return.   The shock cord prevents the trapeze from flying around when not in use, usually holding it just aft of the shroud. The point where the shock cord leaves the deck and the required tension are related: the nearer to the shroud the trapeze is kept, the tighter the shock cord must be to prevent it wrapping round the shroud. If it is too far away the trapeze will obstruct your movement in and out of the boat, but if the shock cord is too tight it will restrain you moving aft and, depending on the set-up, tend to pull the ring out of the hook on the harness.

The shock cord can either lead directly to the ring, or go up to the handle and down to the ring. The advantage of going directly to the ring is that

when you lift your body coming in to tack the ring will come off the hook automatically; but when you do not always have your weight on the wire — typically on a reach when you have the sheet in one hand and the handle in the other — the ring tends to come off the hook when you least want it to. The alternative of taking the shock cord up to the handle means that positive action is needed to take the ring off the hook, which is better when you are in and out with your hands full, but slows tacking, creating a possibly fatal hiccup in the routine; nevertheless I think the latter system is just preferable.

Harness. The harness should support your weight comfortably without restricting your movement. One of the many styles available should be able to do this for your particular figure and weight. There are so many variations in both harnesses and crews that I have no intention of commenting on either, save for some universal points: the hook should be slightly above your centre of gravity, and strong enough (check the root of the hook from time to time, I have found them cracked half through on occasions); remember also that buckles tend to slip when not under load, whereas knots stay put.

Continuous trapeze. Some classes can use a continuous trapeze system where the crew is almost permanently attached to the boat. On the end of the wire each side of the boat are two shaped hooks connected by a shock cord crossing the boat under the boom. A ring or block free to run across the shock cord and hooks carries a strop which is attached to the harness.

This system eliminates unhooking and hooking on when tacking or gybing and greatly simplifies moving in and out of the boat in marginal conditions. These are real benefits, but unfortunately the system can only be used where there is room to cross under the boom facing forwards; the sheets must lead from further forward than usual, which makes it a little more difficult to stay aft in rough weather, and leaves the setting of sheets and guys, for instance when gybing, out of the helm's reach.

There are some important points to consider in setting up a continuous trapeze. The hooks should be as low as the harness and strop allow, so that the block is pulled across the boat rather than down when tacking. The hooks themselves should

Above: a continuous trapeze system. Opposite: trapeze equipment.

have a slight reverse curve leading onto the shock cord, making a shallow dip which is just enough to keep the block from wandering when you're moving in and out of the boat; the hooks are either made from, or end in, a tube containing the shock cord — the difference in the two diameters should be as small as possible so that the block runs freely over the join.

The strop needs to be adjustable to allow some variation in height from the water; the photo above shows a good arrangement, with a block at the top giving a simple purchase and a snap shackle attaching the strop to the harness. Some device is essential which enables instant release when required, but at the same time will not come undone on its own; if the boat is going over you don't want to be fiddling around trying to unhook. The harness itself can have a U-bolt instead of the usual hook — this is much stronger and safer.

Trapezing technique. The most difficult part of trapezing for the beginner is going out and coming back in to the boat; for the expert it becomes no more than a moment's hesitation in an otherwise

smooth movement. If you are just starting trapezing and find it all a bit unnerving, go more slowly at first; cleat the jib and sit on the gunwale, hook on, take your weight on the handle and drop your backside over the gunwale so that your weight is transferred to the harness. Now push out with your aft hand, bring your forward knee up to your chin and your forward foot onto the gunwale; next bring your aft knee up and push out with your forward foot enough to put your aft foot on the gunwale; lean back into the harness as you straighten your legs and shift the balls of your feet onto the gunwale. If you feel unsteady move your feet slightly further apart, but keep on your toes — boxers depend on their balance in the ring, and you never see them standing flat on their feet.

Once you are out on the trapeze, relax, keeping your knees slightly bent to give a little spring between your movement and that of the boat. Your back leg will naturally be more bent than the front so that you lean aft to counter the forward pull of the wire, but never let your front knee lock straight. With practice you will be able to put your feet closer together on the gunwale and still keep your balance; don't be afraid to move a foot forward or aft if you feel that you're toppling, in fact an occasional step to and fro will be essential in rough weather unless you have your feet ridiculously far apart. One way of improving your technique is to practise trapezing on one foot for as long as possible (not in a race of course), which will develop your balance and anticipation of the boat's movement — afterwards having both feet on the side, even tight together, will seem a luxury.

Trapeze height is all-important; any more height than necessary puts extra horizontal load on your legs, making it harder to keep your balance and hampering the relaxed stance we are seeking. Obviously you do not want to be trailing in the water, although in rough waves it is inevitable that you will clip the top of one every so often — this will stop the boat less than you might think. Remember that you will be higher if you go further aft or further out without altering anything, and also that with most harness designs sitting up on the wire puts your backside nearer the water. This is particularly important when you come in towards the side of the boat in a short lull: keep your torso level and just bend your knees to stay out of the water, and do it early enough so that the boat does not start to heel on top of you. Finally, more height means less power, not because of the minute difference in distance from the centreline due to the change in angle, but because the extra load means your knees are involuntarily more bent and your feet flatter on the side of the boat. Just to be awkward, there are times, mostly in light weather, when it is important to trapeze high so that you don't put too much power into the boat and sail further off the wind as a result.

With a bit of confidence you can move more quickly and easily onto the trapeze, particularly when tacking, by keeping hold of the handle and not hooking on until the jib is sheeted almost home and cleated. This brings the boat back to full speed more quickly and the jib can then be accurately trimmed.

Boat trim

Changes in the boat's attitude in the water — the trim — have related effects: firstly on the balance of the boat, i.e. whether it tends to luff (weather helm) or bear away (lee helm), and secondly on the drag of the boat in passing through the water. The latter is a combination of surface drag — simply the friction between the hull surface and the water passing it — and wave drag, which is the energy taken to generate the waves created by the passage of the boat through the water. The relative importance of these depends primarily on the boat speed and also on the hull shape; for a dinghy the wave drag becomes progressively more significant as the boat speed increases up to hull speed, i.e. as the wave builds up around the boat's quarter, and diminishes again as the boat planes faster and faster. In some boats there is a sudden increase in speed as the boat starts to plane and the wave drag drops, and obviously in these classes it is essential to promote and maintain planing as much as possible.

Whilst the effect of the angle at which the boat is sailed should be well enough known, it is vital

Left: going out on the trapeze. With confidence you can hook on as you go out on the wire. Right: to come in, grasp the handle, ease the jibsheet and move your back leg inboard first, bending your front leg. Use the handle to lift yourself over the gunwale, then unhook.

Above: trapezing technique. Adjust your height with one hand, keeping the jibsheet in the other. Below: roll tacking.

that a crew should feel it as instinctively as if he were holding the tiller, if only because a crew can most easily control the heel. Very simply, heel to leeward induces weather helm, heel to weather induces lee helm, and either carried to extreme slows the boat down; the severity of these effects depends very much on the hull shape, longer or scow-shaped boats being least affected.

Whether you are trying to sail the boat heeled to weather, to leeward or upright will depend on the helmsman's preference, although I think it is worth remembering that a dinghy's centre of buoyancy moves sideways as it heels. This is fundamental to the stability, and therefore a leeward heel increases the righting effect of the crew's (and helmsman's) weight, which in turn increases the power which can be used in the rig. In difficult conditions a boat sailed nominally flat gives a greater margin for temporary error before losing speed, but stability is usually more affected by

fore-and-aft trim than by heel. Bow-down trim will make a boat less stable, reduce wetted surface drag but increase wave drag; it is therefore used when the boat is going relatively slowly in light winds, when the reduced stability makes the boat more sensitive, easier to sail and accentuates the effect of heel. In boats where the bow has any grip in the water, bow-down trim also helps the boat point and conversely makes it more difficult to bear away. Lifting the bow has the reverse of these effects — the boat becomes more stable, less sensitive and suffers less wave drag, which is what you need as the boat goes faster.

The last factor in boat trim — usually in the crew's control — is the centreboard. Now the textbooks say that the board should be right down when closehauled, half up for reaching and almost right up for running; this is fine, but when the board is 'right down' a little bit more or less projecting from the top of the box makes quite a difference to the fore-and-aft position at the tip of the board, and therefore to the amount of weather or lee helm. This is accentuated by the twist in the board under load, which will be to windward at the tip when the board is forward of vertical, and reversed when it is angled aft. An adjustable stop is useful so that at the end of a downwind leg the board can be pushed down to a critical position without too much attention.

To windward the board should generally be brought up a little as the wind increases to reduce the weather helm and to free off a bit; when you start to be overpowered lifting the board will reduce the lateral resistance, increasing leeway but also reducing the tendency of the boat to trip over the centreboard. Even with a daggerboard, lifting it slightly will have this effect because the balance also depends on the relative areas of the board and the rudder.

We have already looked at the centreboard

position when reaching with the spinnaker, and there is another situation when you might differ from the textbook setting: two-sail reaching in light winds. In these conditions surface drag is all-important, and can be reduced by lifting the board almost completely; the boat will make lots of leeway and therefore have to be headed well above the course, which in turn improves the efficiency of the slot and the shape of the sails.

The importance of all this to the crew is that if the boat is correctly balanced the helmsman will not need to use much rudder just to keep the boat going in the right direction, and therefore rudder drag will be reduced. In fact by changing the trim and balance the boat can be steered without using the rudder, so it follows that using these changes at the right time will increase boatspeed.

Above: keep your torso level as you come in for a lull — if you sit up your behind will drag in the water.

Tacking and gybing

The greatest coordination of helm action and boat trim is needed when tacking and gybing; all the elements of balance, steering and sheeting must be correctly matched to achieve that magical tack or gybe that takes no time at all and loses nothing in speed. It is all too easy to arrive on the new tack in a flash, pointing in the right direction but with the boat dead in the water; a succession of tacks, for instance to clear your wind after the start, will show up just how much you are losing on each tack. A series of tacks, with a maximum of say five seconds between the completion of one tack and the beginning of the next, is the best way to practise, and soon shows up which parts of the sequence should be improved.

Roll tacking. All boats respond, to an extent which depends on the hull shape and rig, to roll tacking, in which the horizontal turn is complemented by a vertical oscillation which not only

extracts the last bit of drive from the rig, but also reduces the loss of energy to the rudder in turning the boat. In essence a roll tack begins with the boat level or heeled slightly to leeward; the boat is then heeled over to windward as it turns through the wind so that the maximum heel to the old windward/new leeward side is reached as the bow points along the new course. The boat is then brought quickly upright which pushes more air over the sails and accelerates the boat away on the new tack. This technique is most useful in light winds when the impetus from the tack can exceed the drive normally produced, and the sails are blown into position to make the most of what wind there is.

Different boats will react best to different rates of turn, angles of heel, speed of righting, etc. and even in one boat the best treatment will vary with the prevailing conditions. There is unfortunately only one certain way to get it right — practice,

and more practice. If you can persuade another boat to practise with you then you will both have a measure of any improvements or catastrophes, failing which you can only judge the results by feel and the speed of the boat after each tack.

Gybing. Downwind in anything more than a light breeze the essentials of gybing are keeping control and not losing speed. With the spinnaker up it is even more important to keep the boat steady so that the spinnaker does not wave wildly about, making it difficult both to gybe the pole and steer the boat, and probably collapsing the sail into the bargain. More stability is found by trimming the boat down more by the stern, although this is not as simple as it sounds when you are standing by the mast to gybe the pole — so wait a moment until the boat settles down after the gybe before leaping up. A slight weather heel before the gybe helps the boat to bear away, and a quick righting as the boom comes across will help counteract the sudden arrival of the boom on the new side. (Gybing with the spinnaker is illustrated on pages 30 – 33.)

In light winds, and then only without a spinnaker, a little extra speed can be found by rolling

Above: tacking with the trapeze.

Left: capsizing. If the spinnaker prevents the boat being righted take off the pole and bundle the spinnaker into its bag. Then swim around the stern, lever your weight on the leading edge of the centreboard and climb into the boat.

the boat towards the old weather side as the boom is pulled up to the centreline, and righting again as the gybe is completed. However many people would consider this not to be the "natural action of the wind on the sails" and therefore illegal under IYRU racing rules.

Capsizing

No chapter on boat balance would be quite complete without mentioning capsizing. Indeed everybody ditches sometimes. Although it's annoying, letting yourself get demoralised is quite the wrong approach. A better mental attitude is to think that if it's windy enough for you to capsize, there's

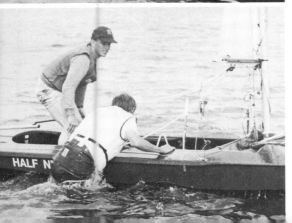

If the boat rolls to weather lie back and pull the spinnaker sheet.

a good chance others will too. Just get upright as soon as you can and get on with the race.

Capsizing to leeward. If you're trapezing and the boat heels past the point of no return, sit on the gunwale, unhook and go straight onto the centreboard. Don't stay hooked on as you will fly through the air and eventually hit something hard; even if you did manage to remain standing on the gunwale, your weight would do no good up in the air and would be more use on the centreboard. If all goes well your helmsman can join you on the centreboard, you can pull the boat up together and sail off.

If you're thrown overboard in the capsize, speed is of the essence to prevent the mast sinking and the boat turning turtle. Swim round to the centreboard and try to climb onto it by reaching up and pulling. If you can't manage it your clothes have probably soaked up too much water — pull yourself up so the board rests under your elbows, drain off and try again.

If the spinnaker was up when you ditched and you can right the boat quickly, leave it up. But if you have trouble, lean in to reach the halyard and pull the spinnaker down. Hold it in a bundle while you climb aboard, and repack it when you have a chance.

Capsizing to windward. There's no excuse for a capsize to windward. If the boat comes over on top of you (usually caused by the helmsman bearing away too much) just lie there. The water will support you, and the boat, freed of your weight, will come upright again — unless the helmsman is exceptionally fat. Keep contact with the boat by pulling on whichever sheet you're holding — this will also pull in the sail which helps right the boat.

**Part 2
Racing the boat**

4 Planning your campaign

In Part One you learned how to become an expert crew. Now you're ready to find a boat and a helmsman and go racing.

Choosing a class

If you look at any class you will find that the winning crews over the years have roughly the same size and shape. Good FD crews, for example, tend to be 75 – 90 kg (12 – 14 stone) and rather tall. Usually there is a small *range* of characteristics, because the boats can be set up differently: the ones with powerful rigs can accommodate heavier-than-usual crews and vice versa.

In general, tall crews have an advantage because when they lean out they exert more leverage. If you're short you may do better in a cramped boat where a tall person's movements would be hampered.

Some boats carry weight better than others. The 470 needs a fairly light crew (and a very light helmsman) whilst a Soling needs a massive middleman. But static characteristics aren't everything — agility is important too. The FD and 505 need crews of the same weight, but you have to be more agile in a 505. As you get older you become less agile but your technical skills should improve. So you may still be competitive in a complicated boat. In middle age you won't win a Windsurfer race but could be a great asset on a Star — though other things being equal the agile crew will always be better.

The heavier the boat the stronger you have to be. When a gust hits an 18-foot skiff it takes off, reducing the strain on the sheets. The same gust will pull the crew of a cruiser overboard unless the sheet is wound round a winch — the boat being too heavy to roll with the punch. Similarly a Tempest is far harder work than an FD although the sails are similar.

So look at the history of each class you're considering and compare your weight, height, strength and agility with those of the hotshots. Although fashions do sometimes change there's little point in starting off in an unsuitable class.

Choosing a helmsman

I have often chosen to crew in my own boats with a friend helming, with noticeably better results than with our roles reversed. So what sort of jockey should you look for?

Firstly, make sure your combined weight is right for the class. Then make sure his strengths offset your weaknesses and vice versa. For instance, one of you has to be good at working on the boat ashore. If you are sluggish, choose a hyped-up helmsman, but if your helmsman is laid-back make sure you can bring him to the boil on the startline. And between you you need, or should have the skill to raise, enough money for the campaign.

In some areas you need a similar outlook to the driver. It helps tremendously if you have the same sense of humour and you must have compatible objectives: a helmsman who is happy with fiftieth place and a win-at-all-costs crew are bound to fall out.

The time and money you will need are interrelated, because you can cut costs dramatically by doing things yourselves. Fitting out and maintaining a racing boat, rubbing down and painting the hull take an enormous amount of time, and will cost a fortune if you have to get someone else to do them. If you're on a limited budget do these yourself, then see how much time you have left and plan your racing calendar accordingly. Decide, for example, if you'd benefit more by travelling to a large number of open meetings or going to one week-long championship.

Although it is valuable to sail often with your helmsman, if you have plenty of experience in your chosen class and have raced a good deal (in any type of boat) you will not need as much time together to reach a good standard as a crew starting from scratch. When Rodney Pattisson and I won a silver medal at the Kingston Olympics we had been sailing together for only six months before the regatta. But we'd both been sailing FDs on and off for ten years and also knew each other's strengths and weaknesses. We decided that a short, sharp campaign would probably be the most successful for us and attacked the Games that way.

If, on the other hand, you're starting in a new class with a helmsman you don't know, take it easy at the beginning. Try sailing together (in any boat) to see if you get on, both afloat and ashore. Aim to have the makings of a team at the end of one season, then you're ready to put together a boat and go racing the next.

Your boat

If you decide to go for a new boat make sure the hull will be stiff, fair and down to weight. Then think about what each fitting has to achieve and choose gear to make it happen. For example, you can adjust the jib leech by raking the mast or by moving the fairlead fore-and-aft or sideways. Whichever you choose, keep the objective in mind and try not to think of the adjustment as an end in itself. Finally, make all the fittings strong enough while keeping them as simple as possible.

If you buy second-hand, try the boat before you make any changes. See how far each system goes towards achieving your objectives. Then if a substantial improvement is possible, modify the arrangement ruthlessly.

Racing at international level, the crews of any class (such as the Flying Dutchmen below) tend to be of similar weight and build.

Fixing your objectives

Establish a common objective with your helms-man. Make sure it is tough enough to satisfy you if you do achieve it; on the other hand, you must believe the objective is attainable. In short, be realistic but stretch yourself.

As well as these 'macro' objectives ("we want to finish in the top five at the Nationals") it helps to have 'micro' objectives too. The pecking order that is established in any fleet after a few races can help here. Subconsciously you may expect to finish tenth (say) and be pleased with a higher place, dissatisfied with a lower. Let's say you decide to buy new sails; your expectations will change too. You will have identified a weakness (bad sails) and believe that removing that fault should make you equal to the guys finishing (say) sixth. Sixth place will be your new target. If it works, sixth becomes your norm and you can go on from there by making another change. If it doesn't the original sails were OK — maybe your tacking is at fault?

Getting fit

The main benefit of being fit is that your concentration is as good at the finish as it was at the start. Your brain can then be focussed on the race rather than on the pain in your legs. Endurance (or heart/lung training) is what is needed here and can be achieved by running, swimming, indeed anything where your body has to work hard for a long time.

Strength and agility are also important: sailing and weight training will make you strong, while squash will keep you agile.

Practising

Winning is one-tenth inspiration and nine-tenths perspiration. You'll need to train afloat to improve both your boatspeed and your boat handling.

You can achieve fair boatspeed by practising on your own. On a beat, for example, try various methods of getting the boat over the waves. Make sure you aren't working against the helmsman. Try to develop a feel for when the boat is moving fast — then you will be able to keep the boat on the boil even when your attention is fixed on the opposition, or on finding the next mark.

Repetition is important when working up basic skills like mark rounding, tacking and hoisting the spinnaker. But make sure you stop every so often to analyse what happened and talk about how to get better, or your twenty quick tacks may do no more than wear through the seat of your trousers.

Paradoxically your practice should also include some racing, as certain skills need to be measured against other boats. For example a 505 can be sailed high on the wind and feel good, but in a race sailing free and fast gets you to the windward mark quicker. So mix practice and racing. And of course, racing is a good way to highlight your weaknesses — to be tidied up in the next practice session.

Lastly, it would be crazy to invest all this effort in your campaign and then have a hot dog for supper, stay up late drinking and arrive at the start too knackered to sail properly. If you want to do well, proper diet and rest are important — whoever said "sailing will change your life" was probably right!

5 Preparing for the race

In this chapter I look at some of the things you can do *ashore* to improve your results. Most of them should be undertaken by both helmsman and crew, so you have double the chance of getting things right afloat.

Sailing instructions

In one FD championship we were halfway down the fleet on the run. Everyone had assumed that the leeward mark was a large buoy used for the starting line, and was sailing towards it. We set off in that direction, but halfway down the leg passed a small, scruffy buoy with 'C' painted on it. After a quick discussion we both agreed the sailing instructions had designated the leeward mark 'C', so we rounded it and started beating. Eventually everyone else followed, but by this time we were well in the lead.

This story illustrates the need for both you and the helmsman to read, understand and remember the sailing instructions: if only one of us had read them we probably wouldn't have had the confidence to peel off in that race. You must also note any revisions to the instructions (usually posted on the race notice board) and take the whole lot out with you.

Make sure you know whether you'll start five or ten minutes after a general recall, or whether there will be a fresh starting sequence. Are you allowed to recross the finishing line (a very common way to get disqualified)? The objective in all this is to be well enough prepared so you don't just blindly follow everyone else.

Tides

Firstly, check the tide tables to find the time of high water. At least you'll then know if you can leave your trolley on the beach!

If there is a tidal atlas of the regatta area, look at the pictures to see which way the water will be moving during the race. Check where the flow is weakest and strongest, and make your race plan accordingly.

Alternatively, look at a chart of the region. This will not only show shallows, cliffs, etc, but should have tidal data giving the strength and direction of flow at various stages of the tide. From this you can make your own tidal atlas of the area.

As a result of all this your aim is to go afloat knowing some general tidal facts such as: "the tide flows clockwise round the bay until two hours after high water when it reverses". Take this information with you — either written down or memorised.

On the course review your data: watch the boats swinging on their moorings or look carefully at the current swirling past marks to see if the expected is happening. The more you can help here the less the helmsman has to do, and that may make him sail a bit faster.

Weather forecasts

Most weather forecasts cover a large area and are of limited strategic use. But the information they contain is valuable and can be used in predicting local winds (discussed fully in *Wind Strategy* in this series). And at least knowing the expected temperature and wind strength and the likelihood of rain or a sea breeze will help you take out the right gear and clothing.

Clothing

Note first that in small boats dryness is irrelevant — provided you're warm it doesn't matter if you're wet (and you will be). So clothing is principally for temperature control — usually when sailing you will be trying to keep your body temperature up, with the wind and water attempting to do the opposite.

Remember that water evaporating off you or your clothes takes a lot of heat — particularly obvious when the humidity is low. In European conditions windproof clothing helps to keep you warm, and you may find light oilskins over a wetsuit are required. In the tropics you might want to use the evaporation to keep cool!

Although I prefer training shoes (for agility), boots will keep you warmer. Gloves are often criticised for reducing sensitivity, which is true — but I maintain your hands won't be sensitive for long if the sheets are burning your skin on a squally reach. So use gloves if you feel they help.

Sort out your gear (including lifejacket and harness) so it causes the minimum of windage — on the trapeze you are right out in the elements and can cause considerable drag.

Weight jackets

Finally, a word about weight jackets. There are undoubtedly times when they're an advantage — usually when you need to power the boat up in, say, medium winds and a slop. They are not, however, a substitute for being the correct weight for the boat, so if you find yourself wearing one most of the time maybe you're in the wrong class. Nor is a weight jacket a substitute for bad tuning — if you're overpowered too often maybe the rig is set up too powerfully.

Personally, I feel the gain in power from a weight jacket is more than offset by the loss in agility, especially in very strong winds. And there is absolutely no doubt that weight damages your back in the long run, and does little for your concentration in the short term. All in all, I look forward to the day when the wearing of weight is banned.

Food and drink

It is a good idea to take some food out to replace the energy you lose during the race, particularly if you have two races in a day. A mixture of carbohydrates is best, including sugar/glucose for short-term energy. The traditional lunch pack of Mars Bars and an apple is probably not far from the mark. But whatever you take, make sure the food is practical (sandwiches are useless when wet) and light. You don't want a full stomach for racing — your long-term energy store should come from last night's dinner and this morning's breakfast — and you don't want your body working hard at digestion when it should be grinding the boat to windward. Simply take out enough for a quick top-up.

Even more important is to take out some drink. You lose a lot of fluid when racing, and if this is not replaced you can become tired without realising it. Take out canned drinks (beware diuretics) or make up your own mixture from the proprietary brands sold for athletes.

Boat preparation

At last, armed with all this food and information, it's time to put the boat together and go sailing. Make sure all the buoyancy tanks are dry and the hatches in place. Pull the bailers up so they aren't knocked off in launching. Be guided by the weather forecast on the diameter of sheets to use and, of course which sails to set — assuming you have a choice. If you haven't at least you're spared one decision!

On the way out to the racecourse set the spinnaker and check the sheets are clear — they should be led outside everything. By hoisting the kite you will also discover whether you have left the spinnaker pole ashore!

When the kite is dry pull it down and repack it carefully, either pulling the sail well back in its chute or covering up the spinnaker bag. A wet spinnaker won't fly properly and you will lose precious seconds after hoisting while it dries. You'll also go faster to windward with a dry — and therefore light — spinnaker in the bows.

Now is also the time to check that the jibsheets and all the other control lines are led properly, and to dry and tidy the boat. Try to spot the windward mark and keep its position in mind during the pre-start period; you will lose concentration if you have to look for it up the first beat.

Try to arrive at the startline early enough to do a test beat. Try five minutes on each tack and watch the compass carefully. Is the wind steady? If not, what is the highest reading and the lowest? What's the mean (average) reading? Is there a pattern to the shifts (does the wind swing right every two minutes, for example)? If you have plenty of time, do several short beats rather than one long one, because you don't want to stray too far from the line. If you do and the wind drops, or the committee moves the line, you may not get back in time for the start.

Setting up for the start

The rig should be set up differently for the start than for the first beat. Your objective is acceleration off the line, and you also want to be able to accelerate (and stop) quickly as you manoeuvre during the last minutes before the gun. To achieve this make the sails rather full — in the case of the jib either rake the mast forwards or pull the jib fairlead forwards from its normal beating position. Later, when you accelerate off the line leave the jibsheet somewhat slacker than normal. These adjustments will give the sail a good draft (for acceleration) and a reasonably tight leech (which keeps air flowing through the slot).

Transits

As you come up to the start, you will find a leeward transit a great help in assessing how far you are from the line.

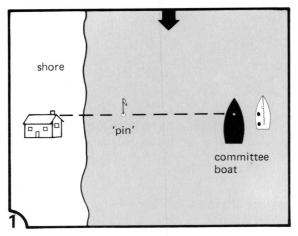

Ask your helmsman to sail slowly past the starboard end of the line while you try and get a transit through the pin-end buoy to another stationary object.

In figure 1 a building on shore lines up perfectly with the pin. So when you come to start you will know you're on the line when the buoy and building line up once again.

Checking the startline

The startline is rarely at right angles to the wind and you want to start at the windward end — the starboard end of line A and the port end of line C in figure 2. To check the line the helmsman sails down it (using the transit to keep on course) while you read the compass. In the example in figure 3 the line bears 220°.

Next the boat is turned head to wind to find the wind bearing. The helmsman watches the Windex (calling "on" when it's lined up fore-and-aft) while you read the compass; in our example the bearing is 320°.

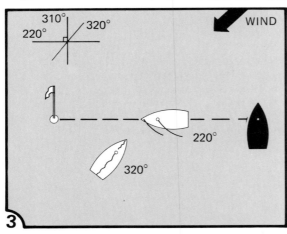

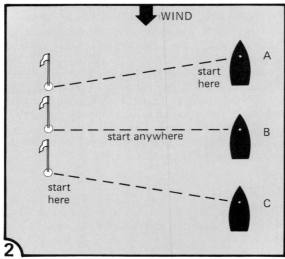

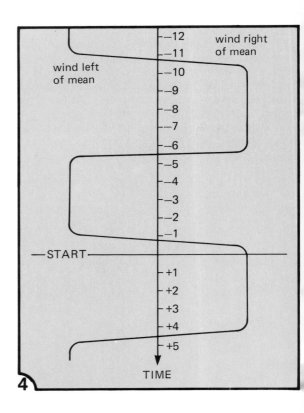

If the wind had been square to the line the wind bearing would have been 310° (220° +90° =310°). Since the wind bears *more* than this the starboard end is favoured. (If the wind bearing had been *less* than 310° the port end would have been better).

In fact it's a good idea to take the wind bearing several times over a period, and use the average reading.

Alternatively, if the wind is swinging to a definite pattern you can plot its progress. Then you can try to be really clever and work out which end will be favoured just after the gun. Suppose, for example, the wind swings right for five minutes then left for five minutes, and so on (figure 4). There are six minutes to go and the wind has just swung left. Most people will start at the port end, but in fact the wind will probably swing right one minute before the start and stay there until four minutes after the gun. So starting at the starboard end and tacking after about four minutes should make good sense.

Checking the start line. Top: taking a wind bearing. Below: taking a line bearing to compare with the wind bearing.

Strategy

Now is the time to check the tide again and look round the horizon for anything indicating a change in the wind — such as smoke, other boats with spinnakers up when they should be beating and so on. Discuss all this with your helmsman and work out your strategy. If you can't make up your mind which side of the course to aim for, maybe you should go up the middle. Although sometimes it doesn't pay to think too hard. I once saw a crew arrive at the windward mark in the lead after taking a flyer towards the shore. "How did you know that side would pay?" asked a mystified rival. The winner thought carefully before replying. "Well, actually, we went that way to watch the girls sunbathing on the beach."

7 The start

Everyone gets nervous at the start. It's a time when decisions are made very quickly so the crew has to react immediately. Starting is an opportunist activity and to get clear air you will need to be flexible in your choice of position on the startline. The luckier you are, and the better you are at manoeuvring, the nearer you can start to your chosen spot.

Manoeuvring

Make sure the centreboard is right down as you line up to start.

To *stop*, let the jib go and push the boom out (but don't hold it out or you will begin to go backwards).

To go *forwards*, pull in the jib leaving the main flapping. The jib gives instant acceleration and snappier control than the main. (Not only is the jib the more efficient sail — it is also sheeted one-to-one.)

To go *sideways*, sheet in the main, leave the jib flapping and pull up the centreboard. You will move sideways without picking up speed — most useful when you are very close to the line.

Calling the time

You must know how long there is to the start, even if the helmsman likes to use his own watch. This is because you have the means of instant acceleration/deceleration — the jibsheet — in your hands. In any case, it would be ridiculous if you had to keep asking the helmsman the time.

In some boats the crew is the only person to have a watch, and calls the time every half minute or so. As the start approaches this shortens to every ten seconds.

Watching the opposition

Just before the start sit in the middle (or on the leeward side) of the boat, controlling speed by sheeting the jib in or out. Face forwards, and keep looking to right and left to check the position of the boats to windward and leeward. Keep your helmsman informed of their positions, and edge forwards as needed to keep in line. As soon as someone else starts to go, you must go too unless he will be way over the line. Watch too for a dummy — the boat next door sheeting in causing you to follow suit, whereupon he stops quickly and you shoot forwards and get your number taken. Of course, selling dummies yourself is highly recommended! If you can get the boat to leeward to move forwards too early, the only way he can stop himself being over the line is to reach off, opening up a nice hole on your lee bow.

Watch out too for boats flying towards the line when you're almost stationary. They may cruise through to windward or leeward of you and ruin your start. If you do see someone coming, tell your helmsman and sheet in the jib — you must be moving before you can do anything. If the 'flyer' is going to tack into the hole to leeward of you, move forwards. If he's coming through to weather accelerate and luff. If he's reaching through to leeward move forwards (to gain speed) and luff. (Alternatively, close up the gap to leeward to discourage him.)

Just before the start

Hook onto the trapeze wire in advance. Build up full boatspeed by sheeting in the jib *gradually* — it feels as though you're squeezing air out of the sail. Don't pull the sheet home fully, but leave it eased about 5 centimetres until you're clear of the boat to leeward. It is tempting to oversheet to try and point high, but all that happens is you slow down and drift sideways.

Similarly, don't go flat out on the wire before the start as this forces the helmsman to bear off to support you, just when he needs to edge up. So go gently onto the trapeze to let the boat luff as she accelerates. Unless the water is choppy, position yourself slightly further forwards than usual — which also helps the boat point.

The first minute

If there's another boat close to weather, don't go flat out on the wire. Your helmsman can then squeeze up without stopping.

If there's someone on your lee bow keep up your speed and try to scallop (luff briefly before coming back on course). If this fails, look for room to weather to tack and also watch the boats ahead so you don't tack at the same moment as them. Relay all this information to your helmsman.

If your start was good, sheet in the jib fully as

Above: sheet in the jib gradually to build up speed as you cross the line.

the boat comes up to speed and move aft slightly to improve speed still further. Trapeze or hike hard to flatten the boat. Keep your helmsman informed but only comment on things that are immediately useful — now is not the time to point out smoke on the horizon. Encourage him to go fast, and never tell him if he isn't! Breathe deeply to help your heartbeat return to normal.

Light and strong winds

At any start you have two conflicting requirements — speed and pointing ability. In medium winds the emphasis is more on pointing, but this is not so in extreme conditions.

In light winds speed is essential, so ease the jibsheet and sit forwards and to leeward.

In strong winds you also need speed to prevent the waves stopping you. Once again ease the jibsheet, but move aft and work to keep the boat flat.

The gate start

Your main objective is to polish the transom of the gate boat going flat out, closehauled and with no one close to leeward. So approach on a fetch, trapezing or hiking flat out with the jibsheet eased 3 to 5 centimetres. As you luff around the gate boat trim the sheet and pump the boat to hold her flat as she turns. Bend your knees, though, if the helmsman leaves the gate boat very close or you may find yourself seated cosily next to the race officer.

Below: manoeuvring at the start. Left, stop by letting the jib flap and pushing out the boom; right, move sideways by pulling up the centreboard and pulling in the boom.

8 Upwind

By far the longest portion of each race is spent beating, so good upwind speed is vital. Although an expert crew really comes into his/her own on downwind legs, there's a tremendous amount you can do to help your helmsman grind the boat to windward.

Trimming the jib

Keep the jibsheet pulled in to its mark unless the boat's speed changes. For example, if you hit someone's wash or the waves get bigger, ease the jibsheet a touch. But if you sail into flat water pull the sheet in past the mark. Similarly, if you want to point higher in the short term — say to squeeze up to a buoy — harden in the sheet.

Wave technique

Your helmsman should be steering a lot to help the boat over the waves, luffing towards each

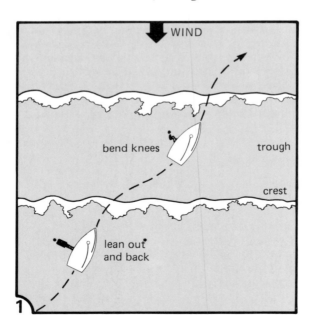

crest and bearing away towards each trough. If he isn't, the following will make him do so! If he is, the same techniques will add greatly to your boatspeed (figure 1).

1   As the bow approaches each crest trapeze or hike flat out for full power, and lean aft. Both these movements help the boat bear away.

2   As you pass through each trough move your body back to its normal station and bend your knees. Both actions help the boat luff.

Just as a skier needs to 'bend the knees' to absorb bumps, it is vital to keep some spring in your legs in case the boat hits a wave badly. If you trapeze straight-legged and do smash into a lumpy sea, the 'snatch' of your weight is transmitted to the boat as a leeward force which ruins her pointing ability. So hang loose at all times, and especially after the start when pointing is crucial.

Relaying information

Once you're in tune with the waves you should start relaying information to the helmsman. Keep an eye on the compass (for windshifts), the horizon for changing weather patterns and study the fortunes of boats on either side of the course. Freeing the helmsman of these jobs lets him concentrate on driving the boat faster.

Preparation for downwind legs

As you approach the windward mark start thinking about the next leg. While on port tack, free the spinnaker sheet from under its reaching hook, and on starboard tack make sure the guy is under its (starboard) reaching hook. Now is the time to remind your helmsman of the compass course for the next leg, or point out the gybe mark if you can see it. Review the tide and check the wind bearing — these will affect your decision whether or not to carry a spinnaker. For example, if the wind has backed and the tide is against you (see

Above: these FDs are aiming high after the windward mark to keep their wind clear before hoisting spinnakers.

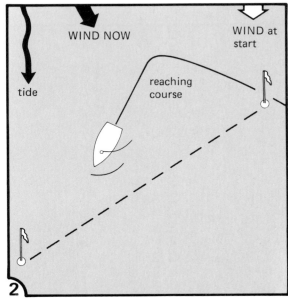

figure 2) carrying the kite on the first reach will be difficult, and it may be best to luff after the mark and set the spinnaker late. Similarly, if you are going to round onto the run and the wind has veered you will probably set off on port.

Discuss all this with your helmsman, while checking the positions of boats around you. He may, for instance, want to luff after the mark to clear the bunch behind before setting the kite. In any case, devise a scheme of rounding so you know when to come in off the trapeze to set the pole.

In light weather you may even be able to get the pole up approaching the windward mark on starboard. If you think this is a possibility, ask your helm to make a slightly longer starboard hitch in to the mark.

9 Downwind

Since the crew controls the spinnaker, downwind speed is largely in your hands.

At the windward mark

Trapeze extra hard to help the boat bear away — come inboard only when she begins to fall on top of you. At the same time sheet out the jib and once you're in the boat raise the centreboard to its reaching position (see page 28 and 42). The helmsman should now bear away still further to stop the boat heeling while you set the pole and guy, since you obviously can't balance the boat yourself during the set.

Wave technique

As the boat begins to surf down a wave, sheet in the spinnaker (to keep the luff just curling) and move forwards. As you climb up the wave ahead the boat will slow down, so ease the sheet and move aft again (figure 1).

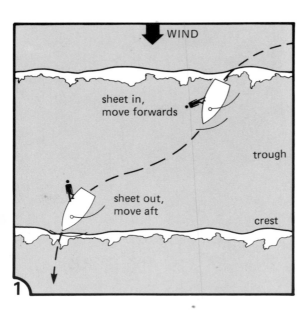

1

If you are having trouble promoting surfing, it can pay to let out some spinnaker sheet at the crucial moment. Somehow the mass of air escaping from the sail seems to nudge the boat forwards.

Pinching up to a mark

On a really close reach you may find yourselves struggling to round the next mark. The first consideration is to determine if the spinnaker is still paying. To decide this simply look at the halyard. The spinnaker is free-flying so the halyard lies in the direction the sail is pulling. If the halyard is streaming out abeam or aft the sail is doing no good, so get it down.

If, however, you want to leave the spinnaker up for some reason, you can make life easier by:

1   Lowering the centreboard.
2   Freeing the jibsheet right off.
3   Raising the outboard end of the pole.

This assumes your spinnaker is housed in a bag. If you have a chute it nearly always pays to lower the sail.

Working the spinnaker

Once the spinnaker is up you shouldn't take your eyes off it. If you decide to splice the Mars Bars, you'll have to locate them by feel! Downhill the expression 'playing it by ear' takes on a new meaning — there's no need to look at the waves because you get quite a different sound from them when the boat slices through a crest than when she rushes towards a trough. So keep your eyes on the kite and use all your senses to help trim it. Remember, too, you should be playing the sheet all the time on a reach, and trimming the guy all

Opposite: usually you will hold the spinnaker until the last moment at the leeward mark, but if you are overlapped (like 11) drop the kite early and concentrate on a smooth rounding.

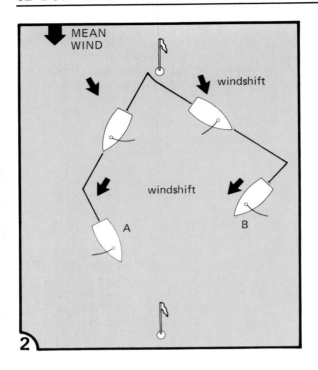

the time on a run. Finally, train your helmsman to tell you what his immediate plans are: if he's going to luff to clear his wind or gybe for the mark, you should be the first to know. That way you can concentrate on the kite 100 per cent.

Lowering the spinnaker

Your practice sessions should have given you an idea of how long it will take you to get the kite down. The helmsman must leave to you the decision about when to lower, unless he has some tactical scheme in mind such as holding on until the last moment to get an overlap.

The run

Tacking downwind will increase your speed considerably on the run. This means you broad reach one way, gybe, broad reach back and so on. How far you go off the rhumb line depends on the wind strength — you need to deviate most in light winds.

Ideally you should gybe on windshifts. These

are hard for the helmsman to spot on the run, and the spinnaker pole is the most sensitive detector: in a header you have to let the pole swing forwards, while in a lift you pull it aft. So relay this movement to the helmsman so he can gybe on the lifts.

In figure 2 boat A gybes correctly on the shifts and gains ground on B.

In very light airs the boat will die if she's forced to bear away too much, so when the spinnaker's shoulders fall in and the sheet goes dead get the helmsman to luff a little to bring the boat back up to speed. He can then bear off a bit until speed drops, when the whole process is repeated.

op row: on a light-weather run you must keep the pinnaker pulling but without sailing too much extra istance. When the spinnaker begins to collapse, ask the elmsman to head up (which brings the apparent wind rward) to fill the spinnaker; once you have regained peed bear away back on course.

10   The finish

Everyone's natural inclination is to switch off up the last beat. It follows that you can make up places at the finish while the other crews daydream.

It's important to know the sailing instructions so you know where to finish: sometimes the finish line is dead to windward of the leeward mark, sometimes it's between the committee boat and the windward mark, and so on.

As you approach the finish it's the crew's job to

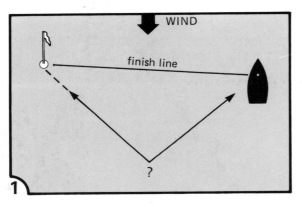

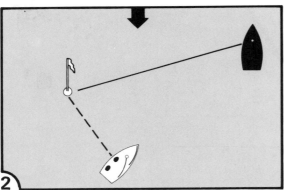

assess which end of the line lies to leeward, that being the end you want to go for. In figure 1, finishing at the committee boat end would save sailing the distance shown by the dotted line. To find the leeward end, beat towards one end of the line. At the moment you cross the lay line to the other end, judge which end is nearer. In figure 2 for example, the pin is nearer, so you should tack and finish right by the buoy.

This is the only reliable method for assessing the finish; often when some distance from the line, I have reckoned that one end was favoured only to find the opposite when I got close enough to use this method.

Keep an eye open for boats coming in from the extremities of the course — it's very easy to concentrate on one rival and ignore people on the edges. The idea is to stay between the bulk of the opposition and the line. Try to keep calm, though and do avoid tacking too often in the last few moments.

As you go for the line it may pay to crack off a bit for speed. Remember to keep going until you have cleared the line, and to prevent your helmsman recrossing it on the way home, as this normally results in disqualification.

As you sail back try not to turn off completely because it's all too easy to damage the boat by capsizing, colliding or running aground. And that means you've got to miss out during the evening while you repair the wretched thing.

Finally, why not give a few words of praise to your helmsman, even if he's done badly? Try not to tell him where he went wrong (unless asked). But if he's been a real pig you could get the message across by standing up in the boat, bowing and saying "Thank you, *sir*". At least this gives you the last word. And that's something every crew likes.